Items should be returned on or before the last date shown below. Items not already requested by other borrowers may be renewed in person, in writing or by telephone. To renew give the date due and the number on the barcode label. To renew online a PIN is required. This can be requested at your local library.
Renew online @ **www.dublincitypubliclibraries.ie**
Fines charged for overdue items will include postage incurred in recovery. Damage to or loss of items will be charged to the borrower.

Leabharlanna Poiblí Chathair Bhaile Átha Cliath
Dublin City Public Libraries

Baile Átha Cliath
Dublin City

Date Due	Date Due	Date Due
2 5 SEP 2013		
17 oct 2013		
0 1 MAR 2014		

The following titles are available at Levels 2, 3 and 4:

Level 2

The Birds
Breakfast at Tiffany's
The Canterville Ghost and the Model
  Millionaire
Chocky
The Diary
Don't Look Behind You
Don't Look Now
Emily
Flour Babies
The Fox
Free Willy
The Ghost of Genny Castle
Grandad's Eleven
Jumanji
The Lady in the Lake
Money to Burn
Persuasion
The Railway Children
The Room in the Tower and Other
  Ghost Stories
The Sheep-Pig
Simply Suspense
Treasure Island
Under the Greenwood Tree
The Wave
We Are All Guilty
The Weirdo

Level 3

Black Beauty
The Black Cat and Other Stories
The Book of Heroic Failures
Braveheart
Calling All Monsters
A Catskill Eagle
Channel Runner
The Darling Buds of May
Dubliners
Earthdark
Eraser
Forrest Gump
The Fugitive
Get Shorty
Jane Eyre
King Solomon's Mines

Madame Doubtfire
The Man with Two Shadows and Other
  Ghost Stories
More Heroic Failures
Mrs Dalloway
My Fair Lady
My Family and Other Animals
Not a Penny More, Not a Penny Less
The Portrait of a Lady
Rain Man
The Reluctant Queen
Santorini
Sense and Sensibility
Sherlock Holmes and the Mystery of
  Boscombe Pool
St Agnes' Stand
StarGate
Summer of My German Soldier
The Thirty-nine Steps
Thunder Point
Time Bird
The Turn of the Screw
Twice Shy

Level 4

The Boys from Brazil
The Breathing Method
The Burden of Proof
The Client
The Danger
Detective Work
The Doll's House and Other Stories
Dracula
Far from the Madding Crowd
Farewell, My Lovely
Glitz
Gone with the Wind, Part 1
Gone with the Wind, Part 2
The House of Stairs
The Locked Room and Other Horror
  Stories
The Mill on the Floss
The Mosquito Coast
The Picture of Dorian Gray
Seven
Strangers on a Train
White Fang

For a complete list of the titles available in the Penguin Readers series please write to the following address for a catalogue: Penguin ELT Marketing Department, Penguin Books Ltd, 27 Wrights Lane, London W8 5TZ

BOOKS SHOULD BE RETURNED ON OR BEFORE THE LAST DATE
SHOWN BELOW. BOOKS NOT ALREADY REQUESTED BY OTHER
READERS MAY BE RENEWED BY PERSONAL APPLICATION, BY
WRITING, OR BY TELEPHONE. TO RENEW, <u>GIVE THE DATE DUE
AND THE NUMBER ON THE BARCODE LABEL.</u>

FINES CHARGED FOR OVERDUE BOOKS WILL INCLUDE POSTAGE
INCURRED IN RECOVERY. DAMAGE TO, OR LOSS OF, BOOKS
WILL BE CHARGED TO THE BORROWER.

Leabharlanna Poiblí Bárdas Atha Cliath
Dublin Corporation Public Libraries

DATE DUE	DATE DUE	DATE DUE
- 4 MAY 2007		
3 0 JUN 2007		
1 3 SEP 2007		
1 5 FEB 2013		

ELIZABETH GASKELL

Level 3

Retold by J. Y. K. Kerr
Series Editor: Derek Strange

PENGUIN BOOKS

To the teacher:

In addition to all the language forms of Levels One and Two, which are used again at this level of the series, the main verb forms and tenses used at Level Three are:

- past continuous verbs, present perfect simple verbs, conditional clauses (using the 'first' or 'open future' conditional), question tags and further common phrasal verbs
- modal verbs: *have* (*got*) *to* and *don't have to* (to express obligation), *need to* and *needn't* (to express necessity), *could* and *was able to* (to describe past ability), *could* and *would* (in offers and polite requests for help), and *shall* (for future plans, offers and suggestions).

Also used are:

- relative pronouns: *who*, *that* and *which* (in defining clauses)
- conjunctions: *if* and *since* (for time or reason), *so that* (for purpose or result) and *while*
- indirect speech (questions)
- participle clauses.

Specific attention is paid to vocabulary development in the Vocabulary Work exercises at the end of the book. These exercises are aimed at training students to enlarge their vocabulary systematically through intelligent reading and effective use of a dictionary.

To the student:

Dictionary Words:

- When you read this book, you will find that some words are darker black than the others on the page. Look them up in your dictionary, if you do not already know them, or try to guess the meaning of the words first, without a dictionary.

CHAPTER ONE

The Ladies of Cranford

My name is Mary Smith and I am twenty-eight years old. My mother is dead and I live with my father, a businessman in the big city of Drumble in the north-west of England. But this story is not about Drumble or about my family. It is about a small town where I lived when I was a child and the people who still live there. The name of this place is Cranford.

In many ways Cranford is quite an ordinary place, where few exciting things happen. But in one way it is very special. Here it is the women, not the men, who make the rules. If you want to know what to eat or what to wear or who to have at your party, you only need to ask one of the Cranford **ladies**. For example, the ladies of Cranford think that it is very important to visit newcomers. You must always do this on the second day after the newcomer arrives and you must visit between the hours of twelve and three. Then the newcomer has to repay the visit in the next three days. These visits must be short: never for more than quarter of an hour. You must not talk about anything that matters because there isn't time and, most importantly, you must not talk about money because that is a subject for business people, not for people of good family. Of course, all the Cranford ladies are of good family, or think they are, which is almost the same thing.

Another strange thing about Cranford is that there are not many men about. Of course, there is Dr Hoggins and the Rector* of the church; and then there are shopkeepers and farmers and people like that. But these men are not part of the real **life** of Cranford, which belongs to the ladies and only to them. You see, most of the ladies do not have husbands. Either they are unmarried or their husbands

* The Rector is the head of the church in a small town or village.

1

are dead. In fact most of these ladies are quite old and they are not very interested in men – or that is what they tell us. 'A man in the house gives so much trouble.' That is what the Misses Jenkyns thought, or more truly, that is what they said.

I want to tell you about these two old ladies because they have been friends of my family for many years. When I visit Cranford, which is about four times a year, I nearly always stay at their house, where I can be sure of a warm welcome. Miss Deborah and Miss Matilda are the daughters of the Reverend Jenkyns. He was the last Rector of Cranford Church – I mean the Rector before the one who we have now. Mr Jenkyns has been dead for many years but both the ladies are very proud of their father and always speak of him lovingly and with great seriousness. Neither Miss Deborah nor Miss Matty (as most people call her) is married but they are important people in the little world that is Cranford. I have heard that Miss Matty did have a male friend when she was young but we shall return to that subject later. Miss Deborah is the one who looks after the house and the money and gives all the orders: she is one of those strong people who knows that she is always right. Miss Matty is quite different – loving, sweet and shy. She is often unsure about all sorts of things and prefers to follow her older sister's rules. They are both good people and everyone in Cranford loves them.

About this time a new family came to live in the town. Captain Brown served as a soldier for most of his life. He was now over sixty years old and had a desk job with the railway that ran through the neighbourhood of Cranford on its way to Drumble and the north. His wife was dead and he had two daughters, both unmarried. The first one, Miss Mary, was about forty years old and was always in bad health, which made her look much older than she really was. Her sister Jessie was about ten years younger and twenty times prettier than her sister, with clear blue eyes and soft brown hair. She spent all her time looking after Mary, doing everything possible to make her sick sister's life pleasanter.

Captain Brown and his daughters lived in a small house just outside the town. They had very little money but the Captain made no secret of being poor. Of course the Cranford ladies thought that this was **shocking**. As I have explained, one of their rules was never to talk about money, and it was unthinkable to talk about not having enough. The Captain again surprised everyone when, one winter's day, he helped an old woman by carrying her Sunday lunch home for her because the streets were icy. In Cranford a **gentleman** did not do this! The ladies waited for him to explain himself but the good Captain did not seem to think that there was anything to explain. He was kind and helpful to everyone, telling Miss Betty Barker what to do when her cow got sick, showing Miss Pole how to stop her sitting-room fire from smoking; so that after some time all the Cranford ladies agreed to forgive his strange ways and asked him and his daughters to their card parties and musical evenings.

But then something truly terrible happened to the Brown family. One afternoon Miss Deborah, looking out of her window, saw small groups of townspeople talking together in the street, so she sent her **servant** Jenny to ask what was happening. Jenny returned in a few minutes, crying and frightened, her face white.

'Oh, Miss Deborah, Captain Brown is dead! It was one of those terrible railway trains that killed him!'

Hearing this, Miss Matty immediately ran out into the street and found the man who brought the news. Soon the railway worker was standing in the Misses Jenkyns's sitting-room.

'Did you see this terrible accident?' asked Miss Deborah.

'Yes, ma'am.'

'Then please tell us what happened.'

'The Captain was at the railway station reading a book and waiting for the train to arrive. Suddenly a little girl escaped from her mother's hand and began to walk across the railway line. Just then the Captain looked up and saw the train coming. He ran on to the line, caught up the child in his arms and threw her up to her mother. But then his foot caught on something and he fell under the train and now he's dead, poor man! They've gone to tell his two daughters the sad news.'

*One winter's day, he helped an old woman by carrying
her Sunday lunch home for her.*

We were all deeply shocked. Miss Deborah looked ill and troubled but she went for her hat at once, saying: 'Matilda, I must go to those girls. They need help.'

Some hours later she came back home, sad and silent. Finally she told us what happened. 'Miss Jessie nearly died of shock,' she said. 'She asked Miss Pole and me not to say anything about the accident to her sister. "Doctor Hoggins thinks that Mary doesn't have long to live," she said. "I'm afraid that this news will kill her." So we didn't tell Miss Mary what happened. She thinks that her father has taken a short journey on railway business and is away for a few days.'

Miss Pole offered to go and stay with Miss Jessie to help her through this difficult time. The next day the full story was in the local newspaper and Miss Deborah asked me to read it to her. When I finished reading, Miss Deborah shook her head sadly and said, 'Poor, dear man. How kind he was. How brave!'

Miss Jessie wanted to follow her father's body to its last resting place and none of the ladies could stop her. So Miss Deborah decided to walk with her to the church. She put her arm round Jessie's shoulder while she was saying her final goodbye to the father that she loved so dearly.

The next day Miss Jessie was again calm and strong. She thanked each one of us with a sad smile. By now it was clear that her sister Mary was dying. Miss Pole and Miss Deborah went to help nurse the sick woman. Mary's last thoughts were of her dear sister and father, and of the great love that she felt for each of them.

'Mary,' her sister said softly, 'our father has gone before you to the place where you and he will rest. Soon you will be together. He knows how much you loved him.'

Now that both the father and sister were dead, Miss Deborah wanted Miss Jessie to come and stay at her house, knowing that Jessie had very little money. But just then a gentleman arrived in Cranford; he was an old friend of Captain Brown and he knew Miss Jessie when she was a sweet young girl of eighteen. This Major Gordon was a fine tall man, about forty years old. He had land in

Miss Deborah put her arm round Jessie's shoulder while she was saying her final goodbye to the father she loved so dearly.

Scotland and so he was quite rich. He loved Miss Jessie and some years before he asked her to marry him; but at that time, knowing how much her sick sister needed her, Miss Jessie could not agree to be his wife. Now here he was again, repeating the same question, and this time Miss Jessie felt able to say yes. In a few weeks they were married and went to live in Scotland.

After she left Cranford, Miss Jessie did not forget her old friends. The two Jenkyns sisters and Miss Pole all went to stay with the Gordon family at different times and came home with wonderful stories of Jessie's house, her husband, her dresses and her beautiful little girl, Flora. In later years little Flora came to stay with Miss Deborah and Miss Matty in Cranford and was almost like a daughter to them. So the sad story of the Brown family had a happy ending for one of the three.

CHAPTER TWO

An Old Love Story

The years went by and Miss Deborah Jenkyns also died, to the great sadness of her many friends. But I continued to visit Cranford, staying sometimes with Miss Pole or more often with Miss Matty. On one of these visits Miss Matty's servant Fanny decided to leave and Martha, a new young woman, came to take her place. In looking after the house, Miss Matty followed all Miss Deborah's rules; but when she had to decide anything for herself, she felt deeply worried and was frightened of making mistakes. She asked me to help her teach the new servant the ways of the house. This Martha was a girl who grew up on a farm. She was hard-working and very honest and she had a kind heart; but she was also a little rough in her ways. She took a long time to learn the house rules. For example, we had to show Martha how to serve food at table.

'You must offer the potatoes and the vegetables first to the ladies and then to the gentlemen,' Miss Matty explained, when her married cousin from India was coming for a meal.

'I'll do everything that you say, ma'am,' said Martha, 'but I must say that I like the men best.'

It was at this time that I first learned about Miss Matty's love story. Her friend Miss Pole had a cousin who lived four or five miles from Cranford. His name was Thomas Holbrook and strangely he did not live like a fine gentleman. He preferred the life of a farmer, wearing old clothes and speaking like the local people. He was a great lover of books and read from them beautifully, with great feeling. He was very much in love with Miss Matty in the old days, Miss Pole said.

'So why didn't Miss Matty marry him?' I asked.

'The rest of her family thought Thomas's family wasn't good enough. You see, she was the Rector's daughter. Thomas asked her and I think she wanted to marry him but in the end she said no.'

'Did she ever see him again?'

'No, I think not,' answered Miss Pole. 'You see, Thomas's house is halfway between Cranford and Misselton. After Miss Matty gave her answer, Thomas always went to Misselton to do his shopping and has only come to Cranford two or three times since then. Once I was out walking with Miss Matty, and when she saw him coming, she ran away and hid.'

'How old is he now?' I asked, hoping that this was not the end of the love story.

'Oh, he's about seventy, I think,' said Miss Pole, breaking my beautiful dream in pieces.

Not long after this conversation, I was with Miss Matty when Mr Holbrook made one of his few visits to Cranford and met his old love again. We were in a shop, Miss Matty and I, looking at some new **cloth** in different colours which she needed to brighten up an old dress. Just then a tall thin man came in, asking for coloured handkerchiefs. I never saw him before. I watched carefully while Miss Matty was talking to the shopkeeper. When she heard his voice, I saw her jump. Then she sat down very suddenly.

I guessed immediately who the stranger was. Hearing Miss Jenkyns's name spoken, Mr Holbrook quickly came across to us.

'Matty, Miss Matilda, Miss Jenkyns! How are you? How are you?' he called out, and he shook her hand warmly. 'I didn't realize it was you.'

He kept talking to us, waving the shopman to one side with the words 'Another time, my friend, another time.' He walked all the way back to Miss Matty's home with us. Miss Matty was just as surprised as he was. It was lovely to see Mr Holbrook's happiness at meeting his old love again. He spoke of the many changes in their lives.

'We have lost your poor dear sister,' he said sadly. 'Dear Miss Deborah.'

Finally he said goodbye but spoke of his warm hope of seeing Miss Matty again before long.

As soon as we got home, Miss Matty went at once to her room and didn't come out again until teatime. When she finally took her place in her favourite chair, I noticed that her eyes were red from crying.

A few days later, a letter came from Mr Holbrook, asking us both to spend a day at his house. He also wrote to Miss Pole. To my surprise, we had great difficulty in getting Miss Matty to agree to go. Finally we pushed her into saying yes and I wrote to tell Mr Holbrook that we were coming. So one Thursday the three of us started out in a borrowed **carriage**, because it was too far to walk. After some time we came to a pretty house with a garden full of roses, standing by itself among fields.

'My cousin needs to make a carriageway up to the front door,' said Miss Pole, while we were making our way on foot through the sweetly smelling garden.

'I think it is very pretty just like this,' said Miss Matty quietly.

Mr Holbrook showed us round the place. He had some fine farm animals. While we walked, he spoke lines from **poems** that he knew. In the kitchen we sat down to a well-cooked meal. After eating, we left him to smoke his pipe. We ladies sat in the sitting-room, full of dancing tree-shadows. There were books everywhere: on the floor, on the table, round the walls.

'What a pretty room!' said Miss Matty.

'It needs a good cleaning,' said Miss Pole. 'Why does he have so many books?'

'Your cousin has always been a great reader,' said Miss Matty.

When Mr Holbrook came in, he asked us to go for a walk in the fields with him but the older ladies were afraid of getting their feet wet. So he took a short walk with me. When we got back, he offered to read us some poems. I noticed that Miss Matty's eyes began to close during the reading. I am sure she was asleep; but when he finished, she woke up quickly and said, 'How pretty.'

'Pretty, ma'am? You mean beautiful,' said Mr Holbrook. 'I will buy you a book for you to keep, because I know you too enjoy poems.'

Finally it was time to go home. Mr Holbrook walked with us to the carriage. 'I'll call on you quite soon,' he said, waving goodbye.

When we arrived home, Martha met us at the door. It was already dark. 'Oh ma'am, you've been out so late wearing only that thin coat, and at your age! What were you thinking of?' she said.

'And what is my age?' asked Miss Matty, with a little smile.

'I think you are nearly sixty, ma'am,' said Martha.

'Oh, Martha, I'm not yet fifty-two,' said Miss Matty in a hurt voice.

After our visit to the old farmhouse, Miss Matty never spoke about Mr Holbrook but I was watching her carefully and I could see that her heart was still true to him.

Mr Holbrook kept his word and soon came to visit us. 'Can I bring you anything from Paris?' he asked. 'I'm going there next week. Oh, and Miss Matty, here is the book of poems that I promised you.'

Soon after this I had to leave Cranford and return to Drumble but I asked Martha to write to me if she thought that Miss Matty needed anything. I did get a letter from time to time. Then suddenly the news came that she was very downhearted and was

Mr Holbrook offered to read us some poems.

eating very little. I decided to see for myself. My visit came as a surprise but I got a warm welcome. Miss Matty really did look ill.

'She has been like this for two weeks,' Martha told me, 'ever since Miss Pole came to see her.'

'And are you happy here, Martha?' I asked.

'Yes, miss, only that I can't have a young man. There's Jem Hearn, a very nice boy who's interested in me. But I promised Miss Matty not to have men friends and I had to send him away.'

When I spoke to Miss Pole, I learned that her cousin Thomas was very ill. It seems that the illness began after that journey to Paris. 'He hasn't been round his fields once since he came back. He just sits at home with his hands on his knees, talking about Paris. Dr Hoggins says that he has not got long to live,' she said.

'Does Miss Matty know?' I asked.

'Oh, yes. She has known for two weeks. I'm surprised that she hasn't told you.'

Miss Pole came to visit her old friend and I left them together. Later, I heard that Miss Matty had a bad headache and was in her room. She came downstairs at teatime and talked a lot about her dead parents and sister, their kindness and goodness and how much she missed them.

The next day Miss Pole brought news that Mr Holbrook was dead. Miss Matty heard the news in silence. I could see that she was shaking and couldn't speak. In the days that followed, she tried to hide how sad she felt by never talking about Mr Holbrook; but I noticed that his book of poems was always on her bedside table.

One evening, Miss Matty was very silent and thoughtful. She asked Martha to come to the sitting-room.

'Martha,' she said, 'you are young.'

'Yes, ma'am. Twenty-two last October.'

'I did say you were not to have followers. But if you meet a young man that you like and if you tell me about him, and if I think he's a good man, I'm ready to change the rule that I made. He can visit you once a week. I don't want to stand in the way of young loving hearts.'

'Well,' said Martha, 'there's that Jem Hearn who is six foot tall and a wonderful woodworker, getting good pay every week. If you ask about him in the town, everyone will tell you he's a very good young man. I'm sure he'll be very happy to come and call on me tomorrow evening, thank you kindly, ma'am.'

Miss Matty was greatly surprised at this reply; but she understood better than most people the importance of love when your heart is still young.

CHAPTER THREE

Poor Peter

One evening we were sitting in the dark, waiting for Martha to bring the lamp and the tea. Miss Matty went to sleep and then woke up suddenly with a strange look on her face. She began to talk about her early life and her father and mother. She disappeared upstairs and came back with a big box of family letters, yellow with age. There were letters from her father to her mother before they got married and letters from her to him. There were also letters from Miss Deborah when she went to stay with friends in the north of England. Miss Matty was specially proud of these letters and read them to me one by one. Finally there were letters written by her father to his son Peter when Peter was at school in Shrewsbury, and Peter's letters to his parents in reply. It was soon clear that Peter often got into trouble. He was usually saying he was sorry for his mistakes. One very short, badly written letter said:

'My dear, dear, dear, dear, dearest Mother,
I will try to be a better boy. Don't be unhappy and get ill because of me. I am not good enough, I know, but I will be good, dearest Mother.'

Miss Matty read these letters to me one by one.

On seeing this piece from the past, Miss Matty felt so sad that she silently gave me the letter to read and began to cry quietly. Later she took this letter to her bedroom to keep it safe, unlike the other letters, which she and I burned in the fire, one at a time.

'Poor Peter!' she said. 'He was always in trouble. Other boys pushed him into it. He loved a **joke**, that was all. Poor Peter!'

Until then I did not realize that Miss Matty had a brother. Another evening, when she was calmer, I asked her to tell me Peter's story.

'His father wanted him to study at Cambridge and then go into the church,' Miss Matty explained, 'but that did not happen.'

'And was he a bad student?' I asked.

'No, that was not the problem,' answered Miss Matty. 'The trouble with Peter was that he was a joker. He loved to play **tricks** on the people of Cranford. Some of his jokes were very shocking. Once he dressed up in women's clothes and said he was a lady visiting the town. After church he asked to speak to our father, to tell him that he was a wonderful church speaker. Father was very pleased, of course, and wanted to give her some of the other talks he was specially proud of. In fact he asked Peter to write them out for her! He never guessed that the unknown lady was really his son and that it was all just a joke. And then a terrible and very sad thing happened.'

Before telling me more, Miss Matty sent for Martha and asked her to go for eggs to a farm on the other side of the town. Clearly she wanted to keep this story as secret as possible.

'I'll lock the door behind you. You're not afraid to go, are you, Martha?' she said.

'No, ma'am. I'll ask Jem Hearn to go with me.'

Miss Matty then began her story.

'One day, when Deborah was away from home and our father was out visiting some sick people, Peter went to Deborah's room and dressed up in her coat and hat – the clothes that she usually wore in Cranford. Then he took a **pillow** and made it into the

15

shape of a little baby wearing long white clothes. Then he walked up and down in the garden, talking to the baby in the way that mothers do. Soon a crowd of people was standing in the road outside, watching him and thinking that he was Deborah. When our father came home, he was very surprised that all these people were looking in at our garden. Suddenly he understood what was happening and got very angry. He pulled the clothes off Peter's back and threw the pillow on the ground. Then he began to hit Peter as hard as he could with a piece of wood. When he stopped for a rest, Peter said quietly, 'Have you finished with me, father?' Then Peter turned and waved to the people who were watching and walked slowly into the house. He went straight to our mother in the kitchen and said, 'I have come to say I love you and will love you for ever.' He put his arms round her and kissed her and before she could speak, he turned and left.

My mother soon learned what happened and went to Peter's room to talk to him but Peter wasn't there. We looked for him all over the house, calling his name again and again. Our mother went on looking in the same places all afternoon but she found nothing. Our father sat with his head in his hands, terribly unhappy, not saying a word. Of course we were all afraid of the same thing: of Peter killing himself.'

'Where was Mr Peter?' I asked.

'He ran away to Liverpool and got work as a sailor. The captain of his ship later wrote to my parents, telling them to come at once to Liverpool to see Peter; but the letter arrived late and when father and mother got to Liverpool, the ship was already on its way to India. Our mother missed Peter terribly. She said very little but Peter's disappearance was a very great sadness and this sadness slowly killed her. Naturally we didn't realize this at the time. She got weaker and weaker, and she thought more and more of the things that she wanted to say to him. By now we all knew that the end was near. She did not live a full year after Peter left home. And just think, on the day that she died, a packet came from India with a big white Indian cloth made of fine wool –

*He walked up and down in the garden, talking to the baby
in the way that mothers do.*

just what she always wanted. We put it round her after she died and I remember thinking that she seemed to have a smile on her face.

Our father was never the same after our mother died. I think it broke his heart.'

'Did Mr Peter ever come home?' I asked.

'Yes, once. He was "Captain Jenkyns" by that time. Our father was so proud of him. He took Peter to every house in Cranford. They were great friends.'

'And then?'

'Then he went to sea again. Soon after that our father died and our lives changed. We couldn't stay on in the big Rector's house with four servants. So we moved to this small house and now we have only Martha to look after us.'

'And Mr Peter?'

'Oh, there was some big war in India. We have never heard of him since then. I'm sure he's dead. But sometimes when the house is quiet, I think that I hear the sound of his feet coming along the street and my heart goes faster; but the feet always go past without stopping and Peter never comes.'

Just then we heard a knocking at the kitchen door. 'There's Martha back,' said Miss Matty. I'll go and unlock the door for her. I find this room much too warm, Mary, don't you?'

Miss Matty left the room. Five minutes later she returned, her face looking a little pink.

'Was it Martha?'

'Yes, and I heard the strangest noise just when I was opening the door. It seemed to me like the sound of . . . the sound of . . .'

'Talking?' I said.

'No, kissing!' replied Miss Matty, and her lips had the shadow of a smile on them.

'I heard the strangest noise just when I was opening the door.
It seemed to me like the sound of . . . the sound of . . .'

CHAPTER FOUR

The Great Brunoni

Soon after this I had to leave Cranford and return to Drumble because my father was ill. I did not have news of my Cranford friends for nearly a year. Then in November I got an excited letter from Miss Matty. The first thing was that she wanted me to buy her a **turban** – one of those hats that Indian men make out of long pieces of cloth – because she heard that well-known people were wearing them that year. The second thing was to ask me to pay her a visit because Signor Brunoni, the famous **conjuror**, was giving a special show at the Cranford Assembly Rooms that week. She did not want me to miss it.

I was very happy to visit Miss Matty again but did not think that a great big Indian turban was right for her sweet little face. She was pleased to see me but sorry that I brought her one of the little hats that she usually wore instead of the much wanted turban.

That evening Miss Pole came round specially to tell us all about her visit to the Assembly Rooms earlier in the day. 'They were full of workmen who were preparing the lights and the furniture for tomorrow night,' she said, in her knowing way. 'While I was looking round, a gentleman who was speaking a very pretty kind of foreign English came and asked if I wanted anything and, when I said no, he showed me out of the room. When I went downstairs, someone told me who the foreign gentleman was – Signor Brunoni, the conjuror! Just then he came downstairs and spoke to me again, so I thought it was time to leave.'

So Miss Pole was the first among us to see the famous man.

'Is he young or old?'

'Is he dark or fair?'

'How does he look?'

Miss Pole spent half the evening trying to answer our questions.

Mrs Forrester was also coming to the show. She was sure that some people were special, able to do strange things that ordinary people do not understand. Miss Pole preferred to look for facts as an explanation. Miss Matty was undecided. After tea they sent me to look for a book about conjuring and Miss Pole studied it so fully that she forgot all about the game of cards that the rest of us were waiting to play. Every five minutes she read out bits from the book:

'A is the ball. Put A between B and D – no, between C and F, and turn the third finger of your left hand over the back of your right hand. You see, Miss Matty, it's perfectly clear.'

Finally we did have our card game but only because Miss Matty gave the book to Miss Pole to take home with her.

The next evening we were all ready a long time before the show. When the doors of the Assembly Rooms opened at seven o'clock, Miss Matty walked in with her head held high, remembering the dances that she enjoyed here when she was young. We sat right at the front. Soon Mrs Jamieson and Lady Glenmire were with us, so we were six. Other people came in and sat behind us but Miss Pole said quickly in my ear, 'Don't look round. It is not the thing to do.' It seems that this was another of the Cranford ladies' rules.

After a lot of waiting, the show began and we saw a wonderful gentleman in richly coloured clothes sitting at a little table. He had a dark beard and a big Indian turban on his head.

'You see, people *are* wearing turbans this year,' Miss Matty said to me softly.

'That's not Signor Brunoni,' said Miss Pole in a loud voice. 'Signor Brunoni hasn't got a beard. Perhaps he'll come soon.'

But the man got up and gave his name in very broken English as the Great Brunoni in person. Mrs Jamieson woke up from her sleep (she fell asleep very easily at all sorts of parties and other happenings), Miss Pole stopped talking for a little and we all watched Signor Brunoni's wonderful tricks. Miss Pole kept looking at a piece of paper she had with her, which explained the tricks, and she went on reading from it in a loud voice. Signor Brunoni looked at

We saw a wonderful gentleman in richly coloured clothes sitting at a little table. He had a dark beard and an Indian Turban on his head.

her angrily but this did not stop her. The rest of us were very surprised and pleased at all the tricks he did for us.

Miss Matty and Mrs Forrester were beginning to think that it was not quite right to watch all these mysteries, so Miss Matty asked me, because I was not a person of the town, to look round and see if the Rector was also in the room. She felt that if the Rector was there, there was no need to worry. I looked and there he was, sitting with a group of schoolboys. He was a tall thin man and people said he was very afraid of women. If he saw one of the Cranford ladies coming down the street, he ran into a shop and hid. At one time people thought that Miss Pole was interested in him; but at the end of the show he gave our group a friendly wave and Miss Pole looked the other way, not wanting to notice him. She was still repeating loudly that the man in the turban was not Signor Brunoni but someone quite different. So ended our evening with the great conjuror.

For several weeks after the Great Brunoni's show, there were stories of robberies, disappearances and other strange happenings in Cranford. I read a report in the newspaper that someone saw the shape of a headless lady when walking one night in Darkness Lane. Miss Matty got frightened very easily by stories like this, and she began to look under her bed at night before getting into it, to see if there was a man hiding there. I'm glad to say she never found one.

CHAPTER FIVE

The Story of Sam Brown

Again several months went by and again I was making one of my visits to Miss Matty at Cranford. Going for a walk one morning, I met Lady Glenmire and Miss Pole starting to cross the fields outside the town. They were planning to visit an old woman who made very good woollen socks. I decided to go with them. We were not sure of the right way to take, so we asked at The Rising Sun, a little pub on the London road. The wife of the pub-keeper kindly asked us to come inside and rest a little, while she went to ask her husband. Just then a beautiful little girl, called Phoebe, came into the room and Lady Glenmire began talking to her. When the pub-keeper's wife returned, she explained that she was not the child's mother and told us a very strange story. Six weeks before, a carriage carrying a big box had an accident just outside their door. One of the carriage wheels broke in several pieces. Travelling in the carriage were two men, a woman and this little girl. One of the men hurt himself badly in the accident and they brought him into the pub and put him in one of the bedrooms. He was too ill to move, so the man's wife stayed to look after him and the other man mended the broken wheel and then went off in the carriage. Miss Pole asked about the sick man.

The pub-keeper's wife replied, 'He's not really a gentleman and he's not really a working man. He's more like a person in the theatre business. The two men are brothers,' she went on, 'and it's difficult to know one from the other.'

Finally we learned to our great surprise that the sick man was in fact Signor Brunoni, and that his real name was Sam Brown. We continued to call him the Signor because it had a better sound but he was no more Italian that I was! From now on the ladies of Cranford decided to look after the Signor and nurse him back to health. Lady Glenmire went to see Dr Hoggins and asked him to ride over and listen to the poor man's heart. Miss Pole promised to find the family somewhere to live in Cranford and paid for it personally. Miss Jamieson sent her carriage to move him and his family to their new home. Mrs Forrester called almost every evening with dishes of food and Miss Matty brought boxes of playthings for little Phoebe. We were so busy with all this good work that we forgot all about the robberies, the missing people and the headless woman of Darkness Lane.

◆

One day Signora Brunoni told me their family story.

'I never find it difficult to know which brother is which,' she explained. 'They do look almost the same but my Sam is a much better conjuror than Thomas. I must tell you that Thomas is a very good, kind person. We were able to pay for our stay at the pub with the money that he's sent us. But he's never been in India and still doesn't know the right way to wear a turban.'

'Have *you* been in India?' I asked in great surprise.

'Oh, yes, for many years. You see, Sam was a soldier and I followed him there. I was happy to be with him but I must tell you, ma'am, that I lost six children in that unhealthy country. Every time one died, I felt that I could never love another. But another came and then it died also. When Phoebe was on the way, I said to my husband. "Sam, when this child is born and I'm strong again, I'm going to leave you. I'll go to Calcutta and somehow I'll pay for my ticket home to England." He agreed, so that is what I did. I walked most of the way to Calcutta and kind people sometimes carried me a part of the way and helped me by giving me money and food. The poorest people, when they saw that I had a baby, often gave me presents of rice or sweets or fruit.'

'But you arrived at Calcutta safely at last?'

'Yes, I got a place as a servant to an English lady in bad health who was going home to England. And two years later, Sam got free of his soldier's life and came home to me and our child. That's when he began his conjuring – he knew a lot of tricks which he learned from Indians over the years. He asked his brother Thomas to help him and Tom has learned some of the tricks, too. The great likeness between the two brothers has helped some of the tricks to work very well when they do them together. But still I can always tell which is Sam and which is Tom.'

'Poor little Phoebe! How far she has travelled!' I said, thinking of the hundreds of miles that her mother carried her across India.

'It's true,' said the Signora, 'and once I very nearly lost her, when she fell ill at Chunderabaddad; but that good kind Aga* Jenkyns took us into his house and saved her life.'

* Aga: an Indian word used for an important man, the head of a family.

'I walked most of the way to Calcutta.'

'Jenkyns? Did you say Jenkyns?' I asked.

'Yes, that was his name,' the Signora answered. 'The same name as the kind old lady who comes to take Phoebe for walks.'

An idea suddenly came into my head. Could Aga Jenkyns and 'poor Peter' possibly be the same person? I decided to do everything that I could to find the answer to that question. I needed more information; but every time that I asked a Cranford lady about Peter Jenkyns, I got a different answer. One thought he was good-looking, another thought he was ugly, one remembered him as dark, another as fair-haired, and so on. The only thing that everyone agreed about was that 'he was probably in India or that part of the world'.

We were so busy talking about the past that we didn't notice something happening right under our noses. One day Miss Pole arrived at Miss Matty's door, shaking with excitement, to say that Lady Glenmire and Dr Hoggins were planning to get married. We all liked Lady Glenmire and felt happy for her; but we were not so sure about what Mrs Jamieson felt about it. Lady Glenmire belonged to Mrs Jamieson's family – everyone thought they were the best family in Cranford – and Mrs Jamieson made no secret of the fact that she did not think Dr Hoggins a real gentleman or his family in any way good enough for hers. Luckily, she was away from Cranford for some days at the time.

'Do you think she'll be pleased when she hears the news?' Miss Pole asked Miss Matty.

'Oh dear! No, I think not,' was Miss Matty's reply and of course she was right. Mrs Jamieson stopped speaking to Lady Glenmire as soon as she got the information.

But the idea of a wedding in this sleepy little town was exciting and started us thinking about new clothes. We were happy to learn that the best clothes shop in Cranford was having a show of all the new spring dresses during the coming week: a great help in our planning what to wear at the wedding.

CHAPTER SIX

Stopped Payment

One Tuesday morning, two letters arrived at breakfast time. One was from my father. In it he asked if Miss Matty still held **shares** in the Town and Country Bank, because there was a story going round that the bank was closing down. Years before, he warned Miss Matty's sister, Deborah, not to put any money into this bank but clearly Deborah did not listen.

'Who is your letter from, dear?' asked Miss Matty. 'Mine is from the heads of the Town and Country Bank. They're asking me to go to a sort of party for the shareholders in Drumble next Thursday. How kind of them to remember me.'

I did not like the sound of this offer but I said nothing to Miss Matty, thinking that bad news usually travels fast.

Instead we decided to go shopping early with the idea of buying half a pound of tea. In this way we could also look at the cloth for the new dress which Miss Matty was planning to make for the Glenmire–Hoggins wedding and perhaps see the new spring dresses before too many of the other ladies arrived.

The young shopmen were ready to show us everything. Miss Matty spent a long time trying to decide between a lovely rose-coloured cloth and a sea-green one. Next to her was a young farmer choosing a present for his wife. Finally he chose the thing that he liked best and offered a five-pound **note** to pay for it. The shopman studied the banknote very carefully – it was a Town and Country Bank note. Then he said, 'I'm sorry but we have only just learned that this bank is in serious difficulties and from now on we are unable to take any of its banknotes. Can you please pay some other way?'

Miss Matty was very interested in this conversation. I tried to bring her back to the problem of choosing a piece of cloth for her new dress but it was no use.

'Young man, I'll give you five pounds in gold for that note,' she said to the farmer. 'I think that there has been some mistake; but I'm one of the bank's shareholders and I'll take the problem to the heads of the bank when I visit them next week. Everything will soon be clear, I'm sure.'

'But what if they give us bad news?' I said, feeling very uncomfortable.

'If I'm a shareholder, I must pay for the bank's mistake,' answered Miss Matty calmly.

The farmer looked at her thankfully and Miss Matty decided to come back to choose her cloth another day. Looking at the spring dresses on show upstairs, we saw Miss Pole across the room but decided that it was not a good time to start a conversation. When we were leaving the shop, the young shopman ran after us and personally warned Miss Matty against having anything more to do with the Town and Country Bank. 'Their banknotes are quite useless now,' he said, with a wave of his hand. 'Don't touch them, ma'am.'

We walked home, neither of us saying a word. After dinner Miss Matty sat at her desk and looked through her bank papers. After some time she shut the desk and came over to sit with me. I put my hand in hers. She pressed it hard but did not speak. At last she said in a shaky voice, 'If that bank closes, I'll lose nearly all my money. I'll only have £13 a year to live on. I'm so glad that dear Deborah didn't live to have these worries. She was a very proud person, you know.'

I could only press her little hand, not knowing what to say.

Late that night I sat down and wrote to the Aga Jenkyns, telling him everything that was happening to his sister. It was the only thing that I could do. If he really was Peter, he was sure to reply.

The next morning the news came that the Town and Country Bank was stopping all payments. For Miss Matty this was the end. She cried a little, not for herself but for her servant. 'Poor Martha,' she said, 'I think she'll be sad to leave me.'

While Miss Matty went to tell Martha the bad news, I escaped

'Young man, I'll give you five pounds in gold for that note,'
she said to the farmer.

from the house and posted my letter to the Aga Jenkyns. When I got back, Martha opened the door for me, crying loudly into her handkerchief.

'I'll never leave her, no I won't! I've got some money in the bank and I've got enough clothes, so I'm not going to leave Miss Matty – ever!'

◆

Miss Matty, when I found her, was very quiet and a little sad. She wanted me to write to my father, asking him to pay her a visit, and I agreed. I tried to think of ways in which Miss Matty could work and get money to live on but she was not a teacher or a writer or a businesswoman. The important thing was that any work that she did had to be 'good enough for a lady'.

Later that same day Martha came in with her young man, Jem Hearn the woodworker. 'We have a plan,' she said. 'Jem and I are going to get married. Then we'll find a house to live in and have you, Miss Matty, to stay with us.'

Jem was a man of few words but he spoke some of them now to Miss Matty. 'I'm thankful to anyone who has been kind to Martha and you have been the kindest lady that ever was. I hope that you'll agree to live with us, ma'am. We'll do our very best to make you comfortable.'

The next morning Miss Pole, looking very mysterious, asked me to come over to her house, where a group of Miss Matty's closest friends were waiting to talk to me. They were greatly worried about how little money she had and had an idea for helping her. Each lady wanted to give some money every year to pay for her living costs but of course Miss Matty must never know about their plan. I thanked them all warmly and agreed to keep the secret.

When my father arrived, I was able to tell him about the ladies' kind offer. In the end we decided on the following plan. Jem and Martha agreed to live in Miss Matty's house. Miss Matty paid them a little money every week for her room and her food. Miss Matty then sold all her furniture and got some more money that way. (I learned later that her friends bought some of her favourite things

'You have been the kindest lady that ever was. I hope that you
will agree to live with us, ma'am.'

and then gave them back to her, much to her surprise.) But the best idea of all was to make the front room of the house into a little shop. Here Miss Matty sold tea to the people of Cranford. Miss Matty was unsure about this idea at first but in fact she was quite good at shopkeeping. She was afraid of male customers because they counted the money much faster than she could and because they spoke in loud voices; but few men came. The thing that she liked best was visits from children and she kept a big box of sweets specially for them!

In this way Miss Matty's life was again calm and happy.

CHAPTER SEVEN

A Happy Homecoming

The ladies of Cranford continued to visit Miss Matty and bought their tea at her shop. Mrs Jamieson was strongly against Lady Glenmire and Dr Hoggins getting married but seemed to find Miss Matty's work as a tea-seller perfectly all right for a Cranford lady. Both Dr and Mrs Hoggins looked wonderfully happy at their wedding the next Sunday and Jem and Martha looked just as happy at their wedding a week later.

The room that Miss Matty used as the shop was bright with new paint, and the words 'Matilda Jenkyns, Seller of Tea' stood over the shop door in gold letters. Miss Matty sold much more tea than anyone thought possible and in fact made quite a lot of money, but she gave away too many free sweets to her younger customers. I came to see her about every three months, to help with her business letters. I spoke to no one about my letter to Mr Jenkyns. By now I was sure it had disappeared on its long journey to India, or arrived at the wrong address, because no reply came.

About a year went by and then suddenly I got a very badly written letter from Martha, asking me to come to Cranford as soon as possible. I was afraid that Miss Matty was ill, so I left home that same afternoon. But the news which Martha had for me was much happier: her first baby was coming in a week or two. The problem was that Miss Matty didn't realize that the baby was near and so Martha wanted me to tell her the good news.

'I don't think she'll like the idea, miss,' said Martha, 'and I don't know who will look after her when I'm in bed having the baby.'

'I'll stay and help until you're able to get up again,' I said. 'Don't worry, everything will be all right, you'll see.'

I left the house by the back door and went round to the front, to the shop, meaning to surprise my dear old friend. The weather was warm and the shop door stood open. Miss Matty was sitting making a pair of socks and singing to herself in a low voice. She stood up to serve me, not realizing at first who I was. But suddenly she dropped her wool with a little shout of happiness and threw her arms round my neck. What Martha said was true. I soon understood that she had no idea of the arrival of the baby. So I decided to leave things to happen in the most natural way. A week later, I again went round to see Miss Matty in her shop, this time with a little baby girl in my arms. Miss Matty was highly excited. Together we looked lovingly at its beautiful little face and hands and feet.

While Martha was in bed getting back to health, I had a busy time cooking our meals, doing Miss Matty's paperwork, looking after the baby and sometimes helping in the shop. When children came to buy sweets, which happened several times a day, I found that Miss Matty always gave them more than they paid for. Really, it was hard to understand how the shop could make any money.

Life in Cranford went on in the usual way. Mrs Jamieson was still turning her back on Dr and Mrs Hoggins: but they were newly married and did not seem to notice anything wrong. Martha was up again and back at work, often with her little girl, Matilda, in her arms. Then one afternoon, when I was sitting in the shop with Miss Matty, we saw an old gentleman go slowly past the window and then stop opposite the door. He put on his glasses and read Miss Matty's name above the door. Then he came into the shop and I said to myself, 'Surely this is Aga Jenkyns!' because his face was brown from the sun and his clothes had a foreign cut. He looked hard at Miss Matty, then at me, then at Miss Matty again. She was a little worried at having a male customer in the shop. The stranger suddenly said to me, 'Is your name Mary Smith?'

'Yes,' I answered.

I could see that he wanted to tell Miss Matty his name but did not want to give her too great a shock.

'Kindly give me a bag of those things there,' he said, pointing to some expensive sweets on the table. Something about his face brought back a remembrance of past times to her heart.

'Oh dear! . . . is it . . . are you . . . can you be Peter?'

By now poor Miss Matty was shaking from head to foot. Immediately Peter took her in his arms and she was crying like a child.

'I have been too sudden for you, Matty, my dear little sister,' he said. It was true. Her face lost all its colour and she was almost unable to speak, so I told her to lie down and gave her a glass of wine. Then I ran to tell the good news to Martha in the kitchen and together we got the tea things ready.

Miss Matty sat opposite Mr Peter at the teatable and could not take her eyes off him. He brought out a dress and some rings which were presents for her from India. Miss Matty picked up the dress lovingly and said softly, 'But now I am too old. Oh, why can't I be young again?'

Peter wanted to stay at a hotel but Miss Matty told him he must not. I gladly gave him my room and moved my things to Miss Matty's room. I left brother and sister deep in conversation and went to make up the bed for the homecomer. Later that night when Miss Matty and I were in bed, she retold some of Peter's adventures: how he fought foreign enemies and ended up a prisoner; how he escaped by saving the life of an Eastern king; how the letters that he sent to England came back with the word 'Dead' on them; how he then decided to stay in India and try his luck as a farmer and businessman. This is where Signora Brunoni met him and where he finally got my letter.

'Kindly give me a bag of those things there,' the stranger said,
pointing to some expensive sweets on the table.

In the middle of the night I woke to find Miss Matty climbing out of bed and disappearing from our room for a few minutes.

'I'm sorry, my dear,' she said when she returned. 'I just went to look at Peter. I wanted to be sure that he is really here.'

A day or two after Mr Peter came home, they closed the shop, giving the tea that was left as presents to the Cranford ladies. The beautiful Indian dress went to Miss Flora Gordon, Jessie Brown's daughter, because the Gordon family too was coming back to live in Cranford.

◆

The house now looked like it did before, with no shop and the empty rooms full of furniture again. Jem and Martha and little Matilda (Miss Matty's name of course) continued to live in the house and to look after Miss Matty and her brother. It was time for me to return to my home in Drumble.

But not for long. A month or two later I got two letters on the same day. Miss Matty and Miss Pole each wrote, asking me to come and meet the Gordons again, because they were now back in England with their children almost grown up. Mrs Gordon (who was Jessie Brown before she got married) wanted to see her old friends in Cranford and was inviting us all to a lunch party at the George Hotel. 'And not only that,' wrote Miss Matty, 'dear Peter is also planning something special for us but he wants it to be a surprise.' And Miss Pole wrote, 'The big question is this, Mary. If the Hogginses come to the party, will Mrs Jamieson also agree to come?' None of us was sure of the answer to that question.

'Leave Mrs Jamieson to me,' said Mr Peter on the day of the lunch. And when we were all at table, I saw Mrs Jamieson beside Peter, and she was listening happily to every word that he said. 'Could these be words of love?' I asked myself. But no! When I walked past their places, I realized that Peter was playing his old tricks again, telling the good lady of his wild and wonderful adventures in the East. He looked at me, closed one eye and said softly, 'This is my way of keeping her happy – and keeping her awake!' We drank the health of everybody in the friendliest way: Mrs Jamieson,

I saw Mrs Jamieson beside Peter, and she was listening happily to every word that he said.

Dr and Mrs Hoggins, Major and Mrs Gordon, Miss Pole, Miss Matty and Mr Peter. Then Mr Peter got up to tell us of the surprise that he planned for that evening. He was inviting us all to a special conjuring show by the Great Brunoni!

That night he entered the Assembly Rooms with Mrs Jamieson on one arm and Mrs Hoggins on the other. And so all was well between the two families in the end.

So now Cranford is a friendly, quiet place again. And dear Miss Matty, a person who loves goodness and kindness more than anyone, is our perfect example. I think we are all better people when she is near us.

EXERCISES

Vocabulary

Look back at the 'Dictionary Words' in this book. Make sure that you know their meanings. Find words that mean the same as the following:

a a woman from a good family
b a piece of paper money
c something which people drive in – horses pull it
d a long piece of cloth that some Indian men wear on their heads
e the time between when you are born and when you die
f something to rest your head on in bed
g a very unpleasant surprise
h a story or happening that people laugh about
i a person who does tricks with playing cards, etc.
j what we use to make shirts, suits and dresses

Comprehension

Chapters 1–2

1 What are the names of these people?
  a Miss Matty's older sister
  b the last Rector of Cranford Church
  c Captain Brown's older daughter
  d Miss Jessie Brown's husband
  e Miss Pole's cousin
  f Martha's boyfriend
2 Answer these questions.
  a What is Miss Matty's full name?
  b How did Captain Brown die?
  c Where did Jessie Brown go to live with her husband?
  d Why did Miss Matty decide not to marry Thomas Holbrook?

Chapters 3–4

3 Say who and why.

 a Who dressed up in women's clothes? Why?

 b Who hit Peter with a piece of wood? Why?

 c Whose face went a little pink after she unlocked a door? Why?

 d Who wore a turban? Why?

 e Who looked round to see if the Rector was at the conjuring show? Why?

4 Who said this, and who to?

 a 'Don't be unhappy and get ill because of me.'

 b '. . . then a terrible and very sad thing happened.'

 c '. . . I love you and will love you for ever.'

 d 'You see . . . It's perfectly clear.'

Chapters 5–6

5 Where . . .?

 a . . . did Sam Brown and his family have an accident? What happened?

 b . . . did Signor Brunoni learn his conjuring tricks? Who from?

 c . . . did Phoebe, Mrs Brown's daughter, fall seriously ill? Who helped her?

 d . . . did Miss Matty offer a young man some gold? Why?

 e . . . did Miss Matty open a little shop? What did she sell there?

Chapter 7

6 Who said: 'I don't think she'll like the idea'? What was 'the idea'? And did 'she' like it in the end? What happened?

7 Who was the 'old gentleman' who came to Miss Matty's shop one afternoon? What happened to Miss Matty's life after he came?

8 Who invited their friends to the George Hotel? Why? And what happened in the evening after this party?

Discussion

1 How do you think the people of Cranford live today, 150 years after Mrs Gaskell wrote her book? What are their 'rules'? How do they spend their time? What parties do they give?

2 This book is unusual because it has no bad people in it. Think of other stories (books or films) that you know. Do you think that stories are more interesting with bad people in them, or less interesting? Why?

Writing

1 In Chapter 1, Mary Smith reads in the local newspaper how Captain Brown died. You are the reporter who saw what happened. Write the newspaper story in about 200 words.
2 Peter Jenkyns loved to talk about his dangerous adventures in the East. Write the story of one of his adventures – in a fight? in prison? at sea? – in about 200–250 words.

Review

Think of a friend or a person in your family who speaks English. Will they like this book? Why or why not?